MASTERING THE
ART OF
TEST TAKING

DR. D. BARNES

Published by Merdels Publishing

P.O. Box 464392,
Lawrenceville, GA 30042
678-859-8902

www.testtakingguru.com

Printed in the United States of America

ISBN-13: 978-0-578-00998-8

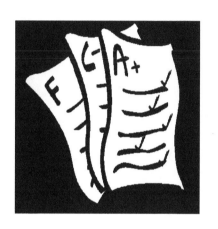

Contents

Contents

Acknowledgements

First and foremost I would like to thank God for making this project a success. I wish to personally thank the following people for their contributions, my husband, Merv, and my daughter Ashley. I would also like to extend my heartfelt gratitude to my sister Vera for her many hours of support with editing, my wonderful daughter-in-law Gillian for coming up with a title for the book, my aunt Roberta, my sons Ramsey and Jonavan for their love and support and, last but not least, my parents Retired Command Sergeant Major Robert Lee Combs and Mary k. Combs for always believing in me.

Introduction

What if there was a proven method of studying that would improve your chances of acing an exam while drastically reducing your study time?

Have you ever taken an exam that you felt you should have done better on?

The truth is **making good grades** on a test is a skill, a skill you can either develop or ignore. People who do well on tests usually aren't any more knowledgeable than people who don't. They've simply developed a certain skill.

<u>An episode in the library</u>

During my first year in college, I spent countless hours in the library. One day, while spending yet another marathon session there, in hopes of **passing an exam**, a fellow student walked by, stopped and said, "Wow—I see you here almost everyday. You must be a **straight A student!**"

I smiled, but did not respond. The truth is, I was barely making the grade.

9

That was the unexpected encounter that changed my life. I really started thinking about my situation. With all the hours that I put into studying, **why wasn't I a straight A student?** I knew some straight A students. I couldn't remember any of them having to study constantly. What did they know that I didn't?

How do the best students do it?

I started looking closely at the people around me. I tried to figure out how the students who did so much better than I did on tests managed to do it without spending all day and night in front of their books. And, *I finally got some answers.*

I learned that there are a number of special test-taking strategies that allow just about anyone to **master the material** that appears on tests.

I used these strategies in my junior and senior years in college to make my studying period as productive and efficient as possible. I had to do better in class and I had to improve quickly.

The results I got amazed me.

The Big Myth

The **Big Myth** tells us that if we don't do well on tests, we have some type of undiagnosed learning disability. Then **the system** turns around and tries to convince your **parents of the same.**

I wrote this book in response to the **Big Myth**, which I know now to be totally divorced from reality. Once I identified what the right test-taking strategies were, I proved something important to myself. I proved, once and for all, that I didn't have some type of learning disability. I also didn't want those who simply didn't have the skills and strategies I discovered to feel that they, too, may have some type of leaning disorder.

The Foundation Principle

You and I are going to be covering a lot of ground together. Before we move on to the specific strategies, I want to share this very important principle with you: **The human brain** is capable of processing far more information than you can ever imagine.

Ask yourself: Who is the president of the United States? What year is it? How old are you? What is your grandmother's last name? Do you remember those things? Of course you do! Did you stay up all night trying to remember them? No. You remember those things because you have grown used to relying on your memory in a certain way... a way that you can and will learn to transfer over into your **test-taking preparations**.

It takes such a tiny amount of effort—and delivers such huge dividends—that I can predict right now that you're going to be amazed at yourself and at what you can do. *You can* become an *expert at taking and passing tests.*

I know this reality may seem unlikely to you now, but I promise you, *it is within your grasp*.

Believe me when I tell you that if you are willing to make just a few very simple changes, you really can unlock your brain's full potential and develop your "memory muscle" with very little effort. Then you can use that muscle to *improve your test scores.*

So prepare yourself for blast-off in T-minus one second ... and then hit "launch" by turning the page.

Chapter 1

Listening Skills

The core study skill is the skill of listening

If you're going to be tested on what you **hear** presented in class, the simplest and most powerful way to improve your grade is to upgrade your listening skills. This is easier for you to do than you think.

I'm beginning the main section of this book with a brief, easy-to-implement program that I guarantee will help you to improve this all-important skill. Below are some tips that will help you to be a better listener.

Seven Commandments for Improving Listening Skills

1. ***Don't talk when the instructor is talking***. It never ceases to amaze me how many students complain about the problem they're having in a certain class and then turn around

and talk, whisper, or pass notes during the teacher's presentation. They have no one to blame for their poor grades but themselves. Don't be one of them. Ever.

2. ***Don't multi-task during the lecture.*** Turn off your cell phone. Turn off your pager. Turn off your iPod. Turn off everything. Don't do work for some other class during the lecture.

3. ***Tune out the outside world.*** Turn off all "everyday" thoughts. Don't distract yourself with internal discussions about what's for lunch, who you will be meeting after class, etc.

4. ***Be an active listener.*** Don't be afraid to nod when you understand something. Don't be afraid to make eye contact with the instructor. If you don't understand the information given, raise your hand and ask for clarification. It is the instructor's job to make sure you understand the information being presented.

5. ***Take part in class discussions.*** If the instructor opens the floor for comments, make sure you are one of the people involved in the give and take.

6. ***Make mental notes of unusual things that happen during the lecture.*** Sometimes, watching the instructor's every move and keeping an eye out for unusual reactions from the class can help you to recall information on a test. For instance, the instructor may have laughed about a certain part of the lecture ... and it might just be the part that shows up on the test. ***Remembering the laughter*** may end up helping you remember the correct answer on the test.

7. ***Come to and be prepared for class.*** You cannot possibly hear what the instructor is saying if you are not in class. Review your notes and do your homework before class. This will make the lecture a lot more enjoyable. Also, use your imagination. Imagine yourself taking part in whatever the instructor is discussing. If he talks about George Washington chopping down a cherry tree, imagine yourself helping George Washington chop down the tree.

If you don't already have good listening skills, then you must use the commandments above to get into the habit of being a better listener. If you follow the ***seven simple principles*** I've shared with you in this chapter, and practice them daily, you will see yourself transform into an exceptional listener.

Chapter 2

Note-Taking Skills

When you consider all the time and effort that goes into the task of recording and retrieving information from your class, you will discover that ***taking notes properly is just as easy as taking notes poorly.*** In fact, once you get the hang of it, taking notes properly is easier than taking notes poorly.

A question for you:

What kind of note-taker are you?

Do you write clearly enough so that someone else could catch up on a missed class by reviewing what you've written? Or ***do you "scribble"*** so hastily that you sometimes have trouble reading your own writing after the lecture?

Do you try to write down everything the lecturer says? If so, do you ever feel stressed and overwhelmed by the difficulty of this task?

When taking notes, ***do you write steadily***, at a measured pace, more or less continuously throughout the class time? Or do you just sit and listen most of the time, writing something down only every five or ten minutes?

Do you emphasize main ideas from the lecture in a special way—by, for instance, circling them or drawing a box around them? Or do you record all the concepts you come across in roughly the same fashion, so that you can't immediately tell, after the fact, which were the main ideas and which were supporting ideas?

Note-taking is an individualized discipline; people do it in lots of different ways, and one person's note taking habits might not work for someone else. But there are some guidelines that should apply to everyone.

Do what the best note takers do

The best note takers are organized and concise. ***They write clearly*** so that they are able to understand the material later. They adopt a consistent approach to taking notes: The notes they take at the beginning of the class are the same quality as the notes they take during the last fifteen minutes of the class.

Choose a format for taking notes, and use that same format when taking notes in every class. Your format should incorporate the subject, a date, the main topic of discussion, and the subtopics that support the main topic.

Don't take a " write it all down" approach. You will spend too much time writing and not enough time listening. However, always write down the material the lecturer writes on the board. This is easy to keep up with, because you will be writing at the same time that the lecturer is writing!

When taking notes, ***don't run your sentences together.*** This makes it harder to study. Just write down the main topic and follow that with key points. Try to do this in outline form. This will make it easier for you to review and recall later.

Example

Look at these two versions of the same number:

574-393-435

574393435

Which version do you think you will be able to re-member faster? The number with the dashes, of course.

Try your best to "***add*** the ***dashes***" (that is, make intelligent divisions) as you are taking notes.

Let's look at another example

Suppose you wanted to summarize what you learned in the last chapter. What would the " bullet points" look like?

They might look something like this:

Topic: "Seven Commandments" for improving listening skills

- ***Don't talk when the instructor is talking.***

- ***Don't multi-task.***

- ***Tune out the outside world .***

- ***Be an active listener.***

- ***Take part in class discussions.***

- ***Make mental notes.***

- ***Come to and be prepared for class.***

Now when you review your notes, all you have to do is quickly read the key points. There is no need to add every supporting point.

Abbreviations

There is another very easy way to increase your speed and efficiency while taking notes. Get into the habit of using abbreviations whenever possible. For the text message savvy, this will make a lot of sense.

Here are some examples

To	2
For	4
And	+
Why	Y
That	t
The	e
In	I
Of	o
Them	m
Into	in2
Before	b4

Some of these abbreviations will instantly make sense to you; others will take a day or so to become **"second nature"**. Get into the habit of using them all, and you will save yourself a lot of time.

Key points

Here's another trick that will help you study more efficiently: Listen carefully to the lecturer for ***repeating key points***. If a topic or subtopic is mentioned more than once, then place a mark by it each time it is mentioned.

For example

> ### *Notes*
>
> ### *Date*
>
> ### *Main Topic*
>
> **Subtopic A 1111**
> **Subtopic B 11**
> **Subtopic C 1**
> **Subtopic D 111**

The lecturer mentioned subtopic **A** four times, subtopic **B** two times, subtopic **C** once, and subtopic **D** three times. Once you review your notes, you will notice that within the lecture subtopics A and D were mentioned more often than any of the other subtopics. That means you should make a point of knowing both those subtopics well. Why are you going to do that? Because it's a virtual certainty that subtopics A and D are going to be on the test!

Using this method allows you to *focus on the most important parts of the lecture*. Prioritize your study efforts around what the lecturer discussed most!

When the lecturer starts a new topic, begin the process all over again. **Keep track of the repetition.** Then, after class, **review** your notes and figure out what you should be studying.

Always **leave a little space between topics** so that, if you have to, you can add more information later.

Reviewing your notes

Review, review, review, and then review some more!

Reviewing your notes on a daily basis is **a great way to study.** You are not studying the material in depth; you are just reading it over. If you have a break after class, use that time to review the material from the lecture you just had. This will keep the material fresh in your mind.

Reviewing should not take more than a few minutes, but you **must schedule** time to review your notes and any related material. For instance, if your notes connect to a chapter in your textbook, then you should review your notes and then **"skim" the related chapter**.

Homework

Taking good notes will make doing your homework a lot easier, especially if a lot of the answers are within the notes.

Comparing notes

Compare your notes with those of another classmate, preferably someone who takes good notes. This can be a mutually beneficial relationship. Working together, the two of you can quickly identify any missed information.

Stay organized

Do not put all of your classes into one book: Use a separate colored notebook for each class. This keeps down the confusion.

Also, use a **full-size notebook**, not a miniature one.

If you remember nothing else from this chapter, remember this: Taking good notes and reviewing your notes daily will keep you from having to cram for an exam!

Chapter 3

Planning a Study Schedule

Planning study time

Time is your single most valuable resource. When planning a study schedule, you must carefully consider all of your available time.

Be realistic. There is no point in setting up a schedule that cannot be followed. ***You must control the way you use your time,*** rather than letting events that occur during the day control you.

Whenever you encounter obstacles or distractions, ***remind yourself of this fact: Your future depends on how well you can manage your time***.

Plan study time every day. Do your best to study at the same time every day. When the semester, quarter or school year ends, then you can take a break.

Follow this rule of thumb

If you are a **college student** you should spend two hours studying for every one hour of class time. If you are in **high school, spend about one hour studying** for every hour of class time, and if you are in **middle school** spend approximately a half hour for every hour of class time.

In order to make this rule of thumb work for you, you must **keep track of every class** you attend. It may be helpful to write down all of the classes you are taking and **the total hours you are spending in class each week**.

Time between classes

Be sure to **make intelligent use** of your time between classes. If you have an hour between classes, make sure you are choosing to do something constructive with that hour.

Ask yourself constantly: Is this what I should be doing with my free time? Will this help me **advance** in my studies?

Studying with friends

Whenever possible try to study in the library. You will find that you get the most done in this environment. **Do not study with friends** unless they are in your study group or class.

Do your homework

When you make your study schedule make sure you include time to do homework.

Always do your homework and turn it in on time. If you don't it could cost you in the end. If the teacher is trying to decide between giving you an A or a B, the first thing he or she is going to look at is your homework assignments. If you have not been doing your homework, guess what: You will get a B.

Sometimes the teacher will put questions on the test that were not discussed in class but were a part of your homework assignment. So again, always do your homework.

Sample schedule

Use the sample schedule on the next page as a model to **create your own study schedule**. Do this weekly or biweekly. Make sure that all time is accounted for, including sleep.

SAMPLE STUDY SCHEDULE

TIME	MON	TUE	WED	THUR	FRI	SAT	SUN
6AM	WAKEUP	WAKEUP	WAKEUP	WAKEUP	WAKEUP	Sleep	Sleep
7AM	Shower breakfast	Shower Breakfast	Shower Breakfast	Shower Breakfast	Shower Breakfast	Sleep	Sleep
8AM	Travel	Travel	Travel	Travel	Travel	Sleep	Sleep
9AM	Math	P.E.	Math	P.E.	Math	Wakeup Breakfast	Wakeup Breakfast
10AM	Science	English	Science	English	Science	Study	Free
11AM	Social Studies	Art	Social Studies	Art	Social Studies	Study	Free
12PM	Lunch	Lunch	Lunch	Lunch	Lunch	Lunch	Lunch
1PM	Physics	Health	Physics	Health	Physics	Free	Free
2PM	Study Hall	Chemistry	Study Hall	Chemistry	Study Hall	Free	Free
3PM	Cooking Class	Music	Cooking Class	Music	Cooking Class	Free	Study
4PM	Travel	Travel	Travel	Travel	Travel	Study	Study
5PM	Study	Study	Study	Study	Study	Free	Free
6PM	Dinner	Dinner	Dinner	Dinner	Dinner	Dinner	Dinner
7PM	Study	Study	Study	Study	Study	Free	Free
8PM	Study	Study	Study	Study	Study	Free	Free
9PM	Free	Free	Free	Free	Free	Free	Free
10PM	Bedtime	Bedtime	Bedtime	Bedtime	Bedtime	Bedtime	Bedtime

This schedule is blank, so you can prepare your own schedule. ***Do it now before you go any further.*** When you have a test coming up, you should be prepared to use some of your free time to study.

WEEKLY STUDY SCHEDULE

Time	Mon	Tue	Wed	Thu	Fri	Sat	Sun
6AM							
7AM							
8AM							
9AM							
10AM							
11AM							
12PM							
1PM							
2PM							
3PM							
4PM							
5PM							
6PM							
7PM							
8PM							
9PM							
10PM							

Chapter 4

Using Charts, Diagrams, Pictures and Graphs

Visual information

Illustrations help us understand compli-cated subjects, but for some reason we are often tempted to skip over them. In fact, my experience is that most people dislike seeing graphs, dia-grams, charts, and pictures in books or on tests. When I was a student, I disregarded them, be-cause they looked time-consuming and compli-cated.

But once I took the time to look seriously at graphs, diagrams, charts, and pictures, I realized how much I had been cheating myself.

Graphs, diagrams, charts, and pictures really do speak volumes. I was amazed at the amount of in-formation they contained and how important they were in helping me to review and *"lock in" key concepts* from a course.

Suppose I asked you to memorize the information below for a test. **How long would it take you?**

States won by U.S. candidates in 2000 election.

Albert Gore	George W Bush
California	Alabama
Connecticut	Alaska
Delaware	Arizona
District of Columbia	Arkansas
Hawaii	Colorado
Illinois	Florida
Iowa	Georgia
Maine	Idaho
Maryland	Indiana
Massachusetts	Kansas
Michigan	Kentucky
Minnesota	Louisiana
New Jersey	Mississippi
New Mexico	Missouri
New York	Montana
Oregon	Nebraska
Pennsylvania	Nevada
Rhode Island	New Hampshire
Vermont	North Carolina
Washington	North Dakota
Wisconsin	Ohio
	Oklahoma
	South Carolina
	South Dakota
	Tennessee
	Texas
	Utah
	Virginia
	West Virginia
	Wyoming

Now suppose I gave you a slightly different assignment. What if I asked you to study the same thing—the names of the states won by Gore and the names of the states won by Bush—only this time, you are to use the map below as your material source instead of the two-column list on the previous page. How long would that take you?

If you studied the map for even a few seconds, you noticed that Gore dominated the **western and northeastern coast lines** and Bush won most of the states in the **middle of the country**. If you know something about the general location of a state, and you certainly do, you should be able to make a good determination about who won what states *without memorizing* an entire map.

Look at the test question below:

Which state did Al Gore win?
A. Arizona
B. New York
C. Kansas
D. Florida

On the map, Al Gore won the **northeastern states** going across to **Minnesota** and only four states on the west coast: **California, Washington, Oregon** and **New Mexico**. Knowing just that information, you can quickly study the map and easily answer the question by the process of elimination. Let's take **choice A, Arizona**. Arizona is in the western part of the United States, but we know that Al Gore only won four states on the west side and Arizona was not one of them. So, Arizona can be eliminated as a possible correct answer.

Now, let's take ***choice B, New York***. Since you know from studying the map that Al Gore won just about all of the northeastern states, starting with Washington D.C. up to Maine, you can conclude that New York could be a correct answer.

But before you mark your answer, you must consider the other two possible choices, which are Kansas and Florida, both of which fall outside of Al Gore's collection of winning states. How do you know that? You know that Gore's total included no southern states, which eliminates Florida. And you know that Kansas is located almost exactly in the middle of the country and was not one of Al Gore's four western states. Therefore the ***best answer is B***, New York.

By focusing on the map, rather than the list, ***you turned two hours of memorizing into ten or fifteen minutes of efficient studying!***

If you spent two hours memorizing which states George Bush won and which states Al Gore won you would have spent a lot of time for maybe **one or two test questions.**

When you spend ***15 minutes on the topic*** you are then able to move on to other things that also might be ***on the test.***

Graphs

This graph displays what activities a student engaged in over a week's time (the graph is based on the sample schedule you saw in the previous chapter).

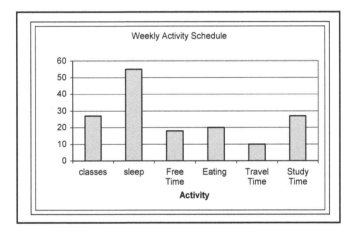

This student spent 27 hours in class, 55 hours sleeping, 18 hours engaged in free time, 20 hours eating, 10 hours in travel time, **and 27 hours studying**.

By examining the graph, you can quickly see that the person spent most of their time sleeping and equal amounts of time in class and studying.

You can look at a graph, **study it for a few minutes,** and easily make a mental note about how the person's time was spent this week. Once you understand how their time was spent, you will be in a **better position to answer any question** the teacher may give on a test about the material.

Pie Charts

Here's the same information in a pie-chart format, which is another effective way of displaying complex information.

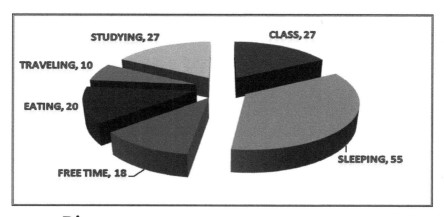

Diagrams

Diagrams make it easier for us to understand the physical world. Many textbooks have lots of diagrams for just that reason: to help you understand, **quickly and easily the way physical objects connect.**

Here's an example of a diagram

If you were preparing for a test and had to quickly revisit the basic principles behind connecting a computer to several components you, would definitely want to spend more time looking closely at a visual aid like this:

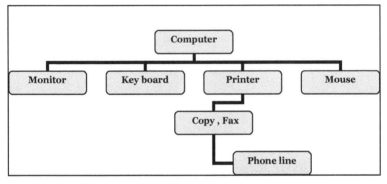

Here's the moral

Keep an eye out for good visual aids as you go through your textbooks and classroom handouts. When you're studying for a test, **always make use of the charts, diagrams, graphs, and pictures and mark them.** If you do, you'll be less likely to **"freeze up", or fixate** on a single topic, and neglect other important things that you should be studying.

If you have completed your initial read-through of a chapter or section in your textbook and have the choice of reviewing long, dense paragraphs of text or studying the relevant graphs and charts that show up in your textbook, which should you choose first? The answer is obvious. You should make a point of reviewing any charts, graphs, diagrams, and pictures first as you prepare for your exam!

Chapter 5

Core Concept

The Core Concept

The **Core Concept** is the primary idea or opinion that the writer is trying to **convey to you**.

It seems obvious, but as obvious as it may be, identifying and drilling the Core Concept of the article, excerpt, problem, or text you are studying is something most people skip. As a result, they spend far too much time *" spinning their wheels"*.

When reviewing study materials, you must constantly ask yourself: What is the Core Concept here? If the author hasn't written out the Core Concept for your benefit, then you must summarize it for yourself.

Once you have identified and reviewed the Core Concept thoroughly, you can rely on your brain to recall the information. Most people are afraid to allow their brains to take over. They feel that somehow their brain is going to fail them, and that becomes *a self-fulfilling prophecy*. Don't fall into that trap.

If you can remember your phone number, your teacher's name, or your favorite actor or actress' best movie, you can remember a Core Concept from an article or a page of text in a textbook. Identifying and remembering information like this is what your brain does naturally. Let it.

When you understand a Core Concept, **your brain does not forget it.** When a question that connects to that Core Concept is asked on a test, you will get it right.

Ask yourself

Find a quiet, private place to study, and you will prove this to yourself. When reading a paragraph, always *ask yourself* about what you just read. Speak to yourself or say it out loud. You're on the right track if you can summarize what you just read in your own words.

If you cannot, then review the paragraph again and ask yourself once again about what you just read. Do this for each and every paragraph you read until you fully understand what you have just read. Your brain will recall the information automatically.

Precondition

There is only one precondition you must meet for this to work. *You must exercise you brain's "memory muscle" by trying to remember things.* Even something as simple as recalling the events of your day before you go to sleep at night will help to exercise that part of the brain.

Here is a study exercise for you. Read the following passage, taken from Wikipedia:

Example 1

One of the earth sciences is Geology. *Geologists* look at the planet's chronology, physical properties, shape, and matter that the earth is composed of. They also check the earth for potential natural resources such as gas, oil, etc. Geologists have a four year degree in Geology or some related field. Their college studies include chemistry, biology and physics.

Use your imagination, your ability to visualize, and your own insights to approach this material. Think about *Geology* being connected to the study of *solid things*. It's not like sociology or philosophy—you have to be able to touch something natural, like a rock or an ocean, for it to be part of the discipline of Geology.

After you have read and reread the passage above, try to use your *"memory muscle"* to lock in what you have just read.

First, underline the key points. (Go ahead— write in this book. It's yours, right?) Then sum up the paragraph for yourself. Try saying its **Core Concept** to yourself or out loud, in your own words, without looking at the paragraph. Do this before you read on.

Your summary should read like this:

Geologists study the age of the earth and what it is made of. They also look for natural resources like gas, oil, etc. They have a four year degree.

There is more information in the paragraph you read, but you only need the main points.

Here is another passage from Wikipedia:

Example 2

Routinely, historians have tried to answer *chronological questions* by looking carefully at written documents. In most cases, historical information can be divided into *three groups:* what is stated, what is written, and what is physically preserved. Historians often stress the significance of the written record.

The expression prehistory refers to an age prior to the availability of written documents.

Again: Use your imagination and your own insights to assess what you just read. ***Underline the key points***. (This is very important; underlining will help you to lock in the material when it's time to review). Then put the book down and summarize the paragraph, in your own words, out loud.

Your summary should sound something like this.

Historical information falls into three groups: written, said, and physically preserved. Prehistory is what comes prior to written documents; history is what comes after written documents.

You cannot summarize every word, and you shouldn't try to. ***Ask yourself***: What is the Core Concept the writer is trying to get across?

Take a look at this last passage from Wikipedia:

Example 3

Biology is the study of living things. Biology includes a wide range of intellectual fields.

The study of ***Biology*** focuses on how organisms act and interact with each other and the natural surroundings, which allows biologists to characterize and classify different species.

You know what to do. **Assess, underline,** put the book down and **summarize** what you just read, out loud and **in your own words**.

Your spoken **summary** should sound like this:

Biology is the study of the characteristics, classification, and actions of living organisms.

Remember

If you can identify and understand the Core Concept of something you're studying, then you can quickly digest that material—and move on to studying other material that you don't yet understand.

Chapter 6

Critical Thinking

Critical thinking

Critical thinking pushes your mind beyond the basic areas of memorization, review, and "recitation"— and into new realms that demand multiple avenues of thought and inquiry. This kind of thinking is an invaluable study aid.

Critical thinkers move away from memorizing and go into analyzing the information under a microscope.

They study the information like scientists trying to discover new ideas.

Critical thinkers conceptualize, visualize, analyze, and then share their information with others. They recognize when things are similar and when things are different. They look for more information on the subject matter and make their own predictions.

There are seven principles that I used in critical thinking.

The Seven Principles of Critical Thinking

1. **Think outside of the box.** Don't take things at face value.

2. **Be confident**. Critical thinkers are very confident about what they know and don't know and they defend their ideas.

3. **Visualize.** Imagine yourself being apart of the information that you are studying. Find as much visual information on the subject that you can, such as pictures, graphs, diagrams, charts, etc.

4. **Analyze.** Take the information given and research it. Become very knowledgeable about the material. With the Internet at your finger tips, that should not be very hard.

5. **Conceptualize.** Use the information from chapter 5 to understand concepts. There will be no stopping you if you can get the concept down.

6. **Criticize.** Be critical of the information given, and compare and contrast it with other information that you may have.

7. **Listen**. Critical thinkers are very good listeners. While they are listening, they are analyzing and reorganizing the information in their heads.

Applying the principles

Consider this math problem:

10 x 2 = ?

Before applying any of the principles of critical thinking, you might assume that the single "answer" to such a problem might look like this:

10 x 2 = 20

But what would happen if you were to look at the problem just a little differently?

Suppose you decided that your goal was not simply to identify the (single) whole number that results when you multiply ten by two, but instead to identify as many of the possible ways of multiplying those two numbers? Your "answer" might then look very different.

10 x 2 = 2 x 10 = 20

10 x 2 = (2 x5) x 2 = 20

10 x 2 = (5 +5) x 2 = 20

10 x2 = ([2 x 3] + 4) x 2 = 20

... and so on.

Critical thinking is more focused on generating interesting questions and points of entry than on generating a single "correct" answer.

I believe that critical thinking activates different neural pathways in the brain.

This kind of diverse brain activity is a very powerful ally when it comes to mastering classroom material.

Multiple dimensions

If you are thinking about oak trees, don't think only of the picture of the tree that shows up in your textbook or the dictionary definition of the word "oak". Look at the oak tree from multiple points.

Think about the tree's root system. Think about the tree's connection with the larger ecosystem. Think about the oak tree's typical height, its branches, its leaves, and the process by which it converts light energy into chemical energy.

In your studies, take the time to ask your own questions about the material you are trying to master. Approach the topic from multiple angles; try to find many different ways of thinking about the same concept.

Chapter 7

Mathematics

Testing well in math

Testing well in math *is easier than a lot of people think*.

Language skills

Contrary to what you might expect, the most essential part of scoring well on a math test is *language skills*.

You must understand math terminology and math formulas in order to do well on a math test.

That may seem obvious, but in my experience, most people *who do poorly* on math tests miss questions because they simply **don't understand the basic terminology or formulas.**

A problem for you

Write a math equation that includes two integers that, when added together, are equal to the sum of one of the *integers.*

An *integer* is any whole number, positive or negative, including zero. -3,-2, -1,0, 1, 2, 3, etc. So, a possible answer could be:

10 + 0 = 10

Now if you didn't know what an *integer* was, you could not possibly have answered the question.

The argument

Some people argue that the simple act of solving math problems in class is enough to ensure proficiency on a math test.

This leads them to set up the wrong priorities when it comes to test preparation. You must first understand the terminology and formulas the teacher will be using to structure the exam.

I took college algebra more than 20 years ago and I can still remember how to work out algebra problems. Why? Because I studied the key terms and formulas first.

Math tips

Read the material first

Give yourself a head start! Reading the material before it is presented in class will help you to better understand the lecture, and give you a chance to **ask questions** about things that you don't understand.

Math chapters are pretty short; most of their content is problem solving. Reading and re-reading a chapter, if necessary, should not take very long.

I **strongly recommend** investing in a second math book written for the same grade level and using it as a reference. Sometimes seeing the same topic written by a different author can help you understand problems that you might find confusing in the primary book.

Formulas and symbols

Memorize all formulas and symbols and underline all vocabulary words. To do this, you should write all formulas and symbols out and include an explanation of how and when to use them. Do the same for all of the new vocabulary words you encounter in the chapter.

Don't try and solve any problems before you completely understand all of the terminology and formulas that connect to what you are supposed to do. Working out the math problem will then be the easy part!

Index cards

Write vocabulary words and formulas on index cards and review them daily. Write the equation or the vocabulary word on the front of the card and the solution to the equation or the definition of the word on the back of the card.

Solve example problems first

Read the examples given in each chapter and try and solve the problems as you go along. The solution to each problem is usually found right below the equation.

Solving problems

When you solve your first set of problems, write out a step by step explanation of how you solved the problems.

Test yourself ahead of time

In the back of most math books, you will find extra problems. Make a copy of the problems and quiz yourself. Close your book and try to solve the problems.

Review all quizzes

Review all quizzes you took during class at least two nights before the test. Make sure you have the correct answers for any missed questions. Most teachers will put questions on the test that are similar to questions from the quizzes.

Ask your teacher

If you don't understand something, ask! Ask your teacher before, during, or after class about anything that you don't understand. Many teachers will be very happy to help you before or after class.

Tutoring

Take advantage of any tutoring that the school may offer. You should also try to tap into online tutoring and study groups.

Take your time

Work swiftly but cautiously. A lot of people try to finish first. Don't be one of them. Take your time and get it right!

Avoid errors

Read the directions carefully. Make sure you completely understand what you are being asked to do. Double check all answers, and make sure that the number on the test card corresponds to the number on the test question.

Test smart

Solve the easy problems first. Even though some of the questions are harder than others, the harder questions are usually worth the same amount of points as the easy ones.

Chapter 8

Categorizing

Memory strategy

This **simple memory strategy** I call categorizing will change the way you approach test taking forever. Why? Because it's easy, it's fun ... and it really works.

What is categorizing?

Categorizing is a method used when you don't know the answer to a question. It is based on where the question and *answers fall in your notes or textbook.*

Categorizing works because it makes the most of your memory. Take just a few moments now to see how it works, and you will reap the benefits forever.

How it works

Let's say you're taking a test and you get a multiple choice question that you think *you know*

absolutely nothing about. Here's what I want you to consider: If you actually studied and reviewed the material, ***you do know something*** about the question. You know what chapter or what section of your notes the question falls under!

So how do you ***jog your memory*** in a way that makes it easier for you to bring to the surface what you do know about the category this question relates to? Instead of trying to "choose" the right answer based on what you think you "know," take just a few seconds to make some notes that categorize both the question and the answers.

How to categorize

Sometimes just remembering when the topic was discussed in class can help you to match it up with where it falls in your notes or in the textbook. This simple exercise can help you select the correct answer!

First

Think about in what chapter or section of your notes you would find the question given on the test.

Second

Think about in what chapter or section of your notes you would find the answers given on the test.

Take a look at how it might work in practice

Let's say the test question asks you something about **the heart**, but you realize, through categorization, that two of the possible answers came out of the chapter on **the kidney**. You can, in all likelihood, eliminate those two possible choices right away. Even if the remaining responses make no sense to you.

If you have more than one choice that falls within the same chapter or section as the question, you must **decide between them**. Here is where you must concentrate and try to recall which of the remaining answers falls closest to the question in the chapter.

Most instructors will pull the question and its answer from the same section of the book. If you stop to think about it, you'll realize that they have to. In fact, most of the time the **correct answer falls within the same sentence** or paragraph that inspired the question!

So, figuring out where the possible answers were covered in your study materials can be a huge help when it comes to eliminating wrong answers—and identifying the correct answer.

The class

I once took a class that had one test which was administered at the end of the course. The test had only ten questions. If you missed more than two questions, you failed the exam, as well as the class. ***I knew the answer to five of the ten*** questions. But, because I studied and reviewed the material, I knew something about where the other five questions and possible answers fell in the different chapters. That was enough for me to use the process of elimination I've just shared with you ... and I passed the test.

Now let's practice

Question 1

One of the seven commandments for improving listening skills is to ...

    A. Plan study time every day.

    B. Write down every word the instructor says.

    C. Avoid multi-tasking during the lecture.

D. Place the questions and answers in their proper chapters or section of the book.

If you read this far in the book, then you know that inspiration for this question came out of the Listening Skills chapter. What's more, you know that answer A came out of the chapter about Planning a Study Schedule. Answer B came out of the Note-Taking chapter. Answer C came out of the Listening Skills chapter. And answer D came out of this chapter, which is about Categorizing.

Think for a moment about what that means. You know where the question came from in this book. You know where all the possible answers came from, too.

Even if you can't remember **all seven of the commandments**, you know for sure that answers A, B, and D cannot possibly be correct, because none of them come from the same chapter as the question. The only answer that comes from the same chapter is answer C. Therefore it must be the right answer!

Let's try another one

Question 2

A particular kind of thinking advocated in this book pushes you to think of the same problem or issue in different ways and to...

    A. Attempt to answer historical questions.

    B. Upgrade poor listening skills.

    C. See the same picture from different angles.

    D. Get into the habit of using abbreviations.

Where did the question come from? Figure that out before you go any further.

The question came out of the chapter about critical thinking. Well, where did the answers come from? Answer A came out of the Core Concepts chapter. Answer B came out of the Listening Skills chapter. Answer C came out of the Critical Thinking chapter. And answer D came out of the Note-taking chapter.

So whether or not you "know" **the right answer**, the only correct choice is C, because only answer C comes from the same chapter that the question arises from.

Once you get the hang of this *method*, **you will love it!**

Memory and categorizing exercise

Below is a group of words that have some type of association. ***Study the words for one minute***, then cover the page and write down as many of the words that you can remember. In categorizing, try and remember what chapter the subject matter falls within.

Chapter 1

Mustache	Eyes	Eyelashes
Lips	Nose	Cheek
Tongue	Hair	Ear

Of course, you should be able to associate each of the items with the larger subject: ***Things found on the face.***

Below is another group of words. ***Take one minute to study the words*** and then cover the page and write down as many words as you can recall. Again, take note of the chapter.

Chapter 2

Tire	Headlights	Hood
Doors	Windows	Bumpers
Seats	Steering Wheel	Roof

You should be able to associate each item with

parts of a car.

Again, take one minute to study the words below. Then **cover the page** and write down all the words that you can remember. Again, take note of the chapter.

Chapter 3

Apples	Oranges	Strawberries
Grapes	Bananas	Pears
Kiwi	Plum	Pineapples

You should be able to associate each item in this chapter with **different types of fruit**.

We're almost done. Take one minute to study the words below. Then cover the page and write down as many words that you can recall.

Mustache	Peaches	Tires
Oranges	Seats	Hair
Hood	Nose	Eyes

This time, categorize the words. Try to remember which chapter the words came from and place them in their proper chapters.

How did you do? What chapter did facial feature match up with? What chapter did parts on a car connect to? What chapter did types of fruit come from?

With just a little practice, you will become better and better at this ... and ***your test scores will go up!***

You also might want to consider buying "brain fitness" books and games that can help to improve your memory and recall. Whatever method you choose, practice, practice, and practice some more. Then review, review, and review some more. The more you practice and the more you review, the better your recall will be.

Chapter 9

Making the Most of Your Memory

Its hard to overstate the importance of making the most of your memory when it comes to test-taking.

Think of the possible implications. What you remember could very well determine your future career—and what you forget could very well deprive you of the scholarship, the school, the job, or the promotion you deserve!

If you take just a little time to learn how your memory works, you can make it do more for you when test-taking time rolls around.

Long-term vs. Short-term Memory

You can probably recall everything that matters about the major events in your life—your first date, your high school graduation—with little or no difficulty, even if the event happened decades ago. Even minute details are probably still very clear to you.

Your memories of those events are the result of a process called " long-term memory". Of course, there's a counterpart to long-term memory — it's called "***short-term memory".***

This is the process by which your brain recalls recent information and occurrences that do not fall into the "major life event" category.

Unfortunately, most of what you study falls into short-term memory, which means it is eventually forgotten.

In fact, you have to re-study the information and "***lock it in" again***. Why? Because the information is stored in short-term memory.

No matter how well you may have studied at first, you must ***constantly review the material if you wish to overcome this.***

We human beings are, more often than we care to admit, prisoners to the limitations presented by the short-term memory system. And nowhere are those limitations more obvious than when you are trying to master information for a series of tests. This is why I advise people: When in doubt … review, review, and review some more!

The transfer of information

Reviewing the material will help you to **transfer some of the information from short-term to long-term memory**. The more information you transfer to long-term memory the easier it will be for you to recall information ... **and improve your grade.**

Chapter 10

How to Approach Test Questions

Different types of test questions

How to approach different types of test questions is one of the ***most important*** chapters in this book.

There are ***four types*** of questions that are seen most on tests.

1. Multiple Choice questions

2. K type questions

3. "All of the above" or "None of the above"

4. Essay questions

Multiple Choice questions

There is a method to approaching and ***success-fully*** taking multiple choice tests. ***It's easy*** and methodic. All you have to do ***is practice*** this method in the order that I give it to you and ***you will be a big success***.

The Method

1. Cover the choices with your hand.

2. Read the question.

3. Write what you think the answer is off to the side of the question.

4. Read all of the choices and check to see if your answer is one of them.

5. If your answer is one of the choices, then mark it and go to the next question.

6. If your answer is not one of the choices, then jot down something that you know about each choice. This must be done quickly.

7. Eliminate those choices you are sure are not correct.

8. Categorize both the question and the choices.

9. Last strategically guess. Choose the choice that falls closest to the question in your notes or in your textbook.

This method takes practice and patience but I guarantee that your test scores will improve.

Taking a multiple choice test is about ***Strategically guessing*** and that is the key to getting the highest grade possible on an exam.

Example

Long term and short term deal with what?

A. Human memory
B. The Core Concept
C. Summarizing
D. Categorizing

Now, if you look at the question above, the only chapter that discusses Long Term and Short Term is Human Memory. So, choice **A** is the correct answer and it came out of the Human Memory chapter. Choice **B** and **C** came out of the Core Concepts chapter. And choice **D** came out of the chapter on Categorizing.

This process eliminates blind guessing and makes you feel ***more confident at the game of strategically guessing***. If you cannot remember what chapter or section of the notes the information came out of, then try to remember when the question was discussed in class. Do the same for each choice. If some of the choices were discussed at a different time than the question then eliminate that choice. Hopefully this will help you to eliminate some if not all of the wrong answers.

K type questions

K type questions are simply questions with multiple answers.

I used to think ***K type*** questions were the ***hardest*** test questions ***on earth***. Once I understood how they worked, ***I loved them***.

With K type questions all you have to do is find one right answer and eliminate all possible choices that do not contain that answer. Or, find one wrong answer and eliminate all possible choices containing that answer.

Example

Which choices below are a part of the Seven Commandments for improving Listening Skills?

1. Be an active listener.
2. Underline or highlight key points.
3. Don't multi-task during the lecture.
4. Make good use of your time between classes.
5. Graphs are extremely powerful tools.

Possible answers to the K type question

A. 1,4
B. 5,2
C. 1,3
D. 3,5

First look at the choices and try to find at least one right answer.

If you studied, then you know that the question came out of the Listening Skills chapter. Choices 1 and 3 came out of the Listening Skills chapter. Choice 2 came out of the chapter on Note-Taking. Choice 4 came out of the Planning a Study Schedule chapter, and choice 5 came out of the Graphs and Diagrams chapter.

With K type questions, it is **easier to just quickly categorize all five choices** and then eliminate all choices that do not fall in the same chapter as the question. In this case it would be the Listening Skills chapter.

Since you know that choice 1 came out of the Listening Skills chapter and that it is at least one correct answer, you can quickly eliminate B and D as correct answers, because they do not include choice 1.

That leaves you with A and C as possible correct answers. Since A and C also include 3 and 4, you must go back and look at those and see if you can figure out which of the two are correct.

Let's say you know for sure choice 4 came out of the Planning a Study Schedule chapter and would be a wrong answer.

Even if you are not sure if 3 came out of the Listening Skills chapter, you should still choose C as the correct answer, because what you know is that 1 *is a correct answer* and that 4 *is an incorrect answer*— with that information, you can find the correct answer.

And with all that, you did not have to know a thing about 3 or 5.

This method can make you a bit nervous because you are relying on a strategy and not your knowledge, but that is how you approach questions to which you don't know the answer—with a strategy.

"All of the above" and "None of the above" choices are just high-end True/False questions.

You rarely see a lot of True/False questions on exams anymore. That's because True/False questions don't always show your knowledge of the material. You have a 50/50 chance of getting the question right whether you know the material or not.

Instead of including True/False as a choice, most instructors will include a few questions with "All of the above" and "None of the above" as possible choices, as well as "choose two or three from the following choices." All of these types of questions and answers can be approached the same way you would a "True" or "False" question.

The first thing you must do is get a good understanding of the wording. Let's start with absolute and double negative words which must be examined closely when approaching the question.

Absolute words

Look for words that are considered absolute, like "never," "no," "none," "only," "cannot," "not," "always," "rarely," etc. ***These are negative words that make the statement more likely to be false***, Why? Because you can never say never.

Words that are not absolute

Look for words that most likely make the statement true; those are words that establish something as being possible, such as "frequent," "sometimes," "possibly," " generally," "often," etc. When you find such words and you don't know the answer, the chances of it being true are greater than it being false.

True or False?

1. ***All* houses are made of wood.**

The answer to this question is <u>false</u> because it is considered absolute, which means there is no room for change.

2. ***Most* houses are made of wood.**

The answer to this question is <u>true</u>, because it is not absolute and it leaves room for change.

Double negative wording

Look out for double negatives —remember two negatives make a positive.

Example

This double negative

3. It is <u>not illegal</u> to drive through a green light.

really means this

4. It is <u>legal</u> to drive through a green light.

When you encounter one of these questions, take out the negative words and re-write the statement. Re-writing the statement helps you to clearly see that it is a true statement. Both 3 and 4 mean the same thing.

Remember to approach *"All of the above,"* *"None of the above,"* and "Choose two/three from the following choices" the same way you would a True/False question. Look out for wording—and make sure the entire statement is true.

Try this method when approaching the question and the possible choices:

- **Read the question**—and then read the question again.

- **Analyze** and underline every word that can make the statement false.

- **Assume** the statement is true and prove it false

- Remember the ***entire*** statement must be true.

- If you find one thing that is ***not true*** then the entire statement is *false.*

- Place a T for "True" or an F for "False" at the end of each choice. When you finish you will be able to easily ascertain the correct answer.

Example

Which states did George Bush win in the 2000 Presidential election?

A. Georgia
B. Texas
C. Arizona
D. Montana
E. All of the above
F. None of the above

This question is from Chapter 4 and it is easy to see that the correct answer is E "All of the above".

What do I know about this question? I know that George Bush is from Texas so, if I don't know anything else I know he won Texas and I clearly remember him winning Georgia, so just knowing that information—I would choose E. I did not have to know a thing about Arizona or Montana to pull the correct answer from the question.

If the answer you are looking for is a true statement and you find more than one true statement, the answer is "All of the above", even if you are not sure if the other choices are correct. If you are looking for a true statement and you find more than one false statement you must consider that the answer may not be "None of the above" at all but one of the other single choices.

If you are looking for a true statement and you find one false statement, you can eliminate "All of the above," and if you find one true statement, you can eliminate "None of the above."

If you find both true and false statements in the choices then it cannot be "All of the above" or "None of the above". It would have to be one of the single choices

Here is another example of a test question that you would treat like a True / False question.

Which states did Al Gore win in the 2000 Presidential election? Choose two.

A. Massachusetts
B. Florida
C. New Mexico
D. Texas
E. Georgia

Again, go through the choices and determine whether each statement is "True" or "False".

Based on the picture on page 33, Al Gore won Massachusetts and New Mexico.

When you treat these type questions like high-end True/False ones, you will increase your chances of getting more questions right.

Essay Questions

When answering essay questions make sure you have all of the proper writing materials, and follow these tips:

1.   Always write clearly.

2.   Print if your cursive is not legible.

3.   Begin your essay by re-stating the question.

I never considered myself a very good writer, so when I saw essay questions on a test, I would cringe. Once I had a plan as to how to approach essay questions I really started to enjoy them.

The three main parts of an essay

When responding to an essay question, you must always have three main parts:

1.   *Introduction*

2.   *Main body*

3.   *Conclusion*

The wording

There are words to watch for in essay questions. These words will define your answer. Words like "compare", "contrast", "analyze", "criticize", "cause and effect", etc. Get familiar with these

words, so when you see them on a test, you will
know what to do.

The most popular types of essay questions

- **Compare**: Take two or more things and write
  about their similarities.

- **Contrast:** Take two or more things and
  write about their differences.

- *Cause and Effect:* Write how one event has
  an effect on the other.

- *Criticize:* Write your opinion about a topic or
  situation.

Answering the question

*Always have an outline plan for essay
questions*. Quickly outline what you want to say
on a separate piece of paper. *Then write your
actual answer.* This will help you stay organized and focused on the question.

One of the things I like about essay questions is
that *even if you did not know the answer
but made an attempt to answer the question, you could get some points*—unlike multiple choice questions, which are either right or
wrong.

85

If you know the answer, then put it in the first paragraph and spend the rest of the time backing it up.

If I was not clear on the question, I would ask the teacher for clarification and then write everything I knew about the topic, hoping that the correct answer was in there somewhere. ***Remember: Only do this when you don't know the answer.***

In conclusion

When approaching different types of test questions, you must have a strategy. ***A plan always makes things seem a lot easier.*** Study these methods and put them to use right away.

Chapter 11

Putting Old Test Questions to Good Use

<u>Old test questions</u>

When I was in school, I thought reviewing the questions from an old tests was a ***form of cheating***. Then I realized that everyone was doing it and many teachers actually encouraged this method of studying.

I started looking closely at old tests, and it was one of the best decisions I ever made. Reviewing old tests will give you a sense of how the teacher structures the test.

That's what you're really studying: the teacher's test-giving style. That information is ***priceless!***

Don't bother trying to memorize the answers. Some people do this in hopes of seeing the same questions on the test. But what if the teacher makes up a whole new test?

Chapter 11: Putting Old Test Questions to Good Use

Follow these simple rules

Only look at old test after you have studied all the material and feel you are ready to take the upcoming test.

Make yourself an answer sheet and write the correct answers to the test on a separate sheet of paper. Then erase or white out the correct answers on the old test and make a copy.

Next, take the test as though you were taking the actual exam. Try to answer each question, without looking at the possible choices. Write your answer off to the side and then check to see if your answer is one of the choices.

This will also help you practice your test-taking techniques and strategies. **Time yourself** to see if you can complete the test in a timely fashion. Then grade the test and find out how you did.

Now go over the old test again and dissect it. Figure out why the other choices for each question were not correct.

Try and think of everything you know about each choice. This will help you broaden your knowledge of the material.

Next, categorize each question and its choices by placing each choice where it falls in the chapter or section of your notes. Do this even if you already know the correct answer. This practice will help you build stamina and confidence. I have gotten many questions right using this method.

Once you have completed the above task, take the old test again and see how easy you understand the question and all of the possible answers.

If you have to take a test that allows you to purchase sample exams, by all means, buy at least one. Then take the exam as described above and then dissect every single question and answer.

If you purchased a book to study for a particular exam then start studying in the middle of the book and go toward the back first, because most of the information in the first half of the book is stuff you should already know. Most of what will be asked on a test will usually come from the last half of the book.

Remember

Simply memorizing the right answers on an old test is almost certainly a complete waste of your most valuable resource - time. Use old tests to practice your knowledge of the material and *to get a better understanding of how the teacher formulates his or her test!*

This method really makes you use your brain, and it always pays off.

Chapter 12

Note Sheet

Note sheet

A note sheet is information that you write on a piece of paper. It is filled with things you think you might forget.

A note sheet is usually written one to two days before the test, after you finish going over your old tests and your studying is complete.

A note sheet will prevent you from flipping through books and papers the morning of the exam.

Just take a few minutes and write down *formulas, diagrams, and things you think you might forget.* You can use as much of the sheet as you need. But you must be able to *re-write it in five minutes or less.* So, you will have to practice rewriting this sheet the night before the exam.

After several re-writes, you will now have to memorize the sheet.

On the morning of the exam while everyone else is talking, you will be reviewing your note sheet.

If you have time before class, quietly ask the teacher if you can write on the back of your test. Or, ask if he or she has a blank sheet of paper that you can write on during the test.

It is **very important** that you know what you can or cannot do during the test. So, make sure you are clear on what you can do so **that you won't be penalized.**

First five minutes

During the first five minutes of the exam you should re-write your note sheet on the back of your test or on a separate sheet of paper.

Chapter 13

Count Down to Test Day

This is crunch time

You must be organized with your school work and stay that way throughout the semester. Not being organized could cost you in the end.

Make a plan and stick to it

Always have a study schedule, and treat it like a job. Your future depends on it. It will make the difference between you making $8,000 dollars a year or $80,000 dollars a year.

Go over all of the notes, study materials, etc., that you have been reviewing on a daily basis and make sure you understand the concepts.

Go to bed

The night before the test, write out your note sheet and **go to bed on time,** even if you are not finished studying. A tired mind will only make matters worse.

I have stayed up late many times the night before an exam, studying last-minute stuff, and I cannot remember it once ever benefiting me, **so don't do it.**

Below are things you should do before test day.

One week before the test

- **Be clear** on what is going to be on the test. There is no need to study extra material.

- **Work on material** that you don't understand.

- **Make sure** you have all of the lecture notes that are going to be on the test.

- **Get a hold of old tests**.

- **Work with a study group** and get help if needed.

Five days before the test

- **Review** all homework.

- **Work** with study group.

- **Review** all graphs, diagrams, charts, and pictures.

Four days before the test

- ***Start categorizing*** the material as you study

- ***Meet with the teacher,*** if possible, and go over exactly what is going to be on the test.

Three days before the test

- **Get with your study *group,*** compare notes, and go over all the material that is going to be on the test.

- **Review**, *review, review, review.*

- **Review homework, quizzes,** and any previous tests that might be relevant to the test.

Two days before the test

- **Complete your studying** and stay up late if you have to.

- **Take old quizzes** as if they were the actual quiz. Time yourself.

- ***Work on writing*** and rewriting your note sheet.

One day before the test

- **Take the old test** as if it were the actual exam.

- **Go over old tests and categorize** all the questions and answers. This is good practice.

- *Look at each wrong answer* and explain why it is not the right answer.

- **Write out a note sheet** and turn in early.

- *Get plenty of sleep!*

The day of the test

- **Eat breakfast** in the morning if that is what you normally do. If you don't usually eat breakfast, then I suggest you have a light snack.

- **Go to school early** even if the test is in the middle of the day. Take this time to go over things you think you might forget.

- **Do not do a lot of talking** with classmates; this will only make you nervous. Someone might mention something that "they think" is going to be on the test that you didn't study.

- **Try and find a quiet place** in the library to study and hide out.

During the test

Be repetitious on every test you take. Do everything in the same order every time you take a test, no matter what test you are taking.

Here's an example

- *Quietly ask the teacher* if you can write on the back of your test or on a separate sheet of paper.

- Put your **books down**.

- Place your **watch** on the corner of your desk.

- Once you get your test, *turn it over* and **write your note sheet** on the back.

- *Count the number of questions* and divide them by the time you have left.

- **Make sure you fully understand the instructions** before answering the questions.

- Always **cover the possible answers** with your hand and read the question. If you are taking the test on a computer then cover the choices with a piece of paper by holding it up to the computer screen.

- **Write your answer** off to the side.

- **Check** to see if **your answer** is one of the choices.

- **If your answer is one of the choices, then circle it** and move on to the next question.

- If your **answer is not one of the choices,** first eliminate those you know are incorrect and categorize the rest picking the answer that falls closest to the question.

- If answering the question becomes time-consuming, then mark it and come back to it later.

- ***Do not, I repeat, do not be the first one finished***. Take your time and get it right. I suggest you use the entire test period to take your test.

Review your test and make sure if you are using an answer sheet that you have the correct answer in each box. ***Don't lose precious points by making unnecessary mistakes***.

Once you finish reviewing your test and turn it in go some place and relax for a few minutes, especially if you have another class after the test.

The Art of Test-taking

If you practice all of the methods outlined in this book it is almost a certainty that you will be a huge success. By mastering the art, you will become a test-taking guru and you will be successful in all that you endeavor to do.

Chapter 14

Test Anxiety

Most of us get very nervous when it comes
to taking tests.

This is what would happen to me. My **stomach**
would get **upset**. My **palms** would **sweat.** I
would *feel faint*, *jittery, confused*, and sometimes even **panicked**. My **heart** would **beat**
really *fast. A*ll this would happen right before the
test.

I found a very easy way to control about 95% of
my anxiety and I can help you control yours, too.

Here are some simple rules to follow.

Be prepared

Be prepared for the test. Study all related material.
I found that I had the biggest anxiety attacks when
I was not prepared for the test.

Do not cram

Do not cram the night before an exam. Follow the outline in chapter 13 on Count Down to Test Day.

Get plenty of rest

I found that getting plenty of rest helped me to concentrate better and recall more information. If I stayed up late the night before the test, I would feel mentally and physically drained while I was taking the test, neither of which helped my grade.

Do not talk with classmates before the test

Sometimes talking with classmates on the morning of the test can cause unnecessary stress. They might pass their anxiety onto you, or they might mention something that they think might be on the test that you did not study. All of this will increase your stress level.

Don't do a lot of talking with classmates after the test.

Just concentrate on the next upcoming test. Do not lose time thinking about what you might have missed. Just be patient and wait to get your test back. **You will be pleasantly surprised.**

<u>Eat</u>

If you normally eat breakfast in the morning then do so, but if you are not one that eats breakfast then have a light snack. When eating or drinking stay away from foods with high sugar or caffeine content, because this will only increase your anxiety level.

<u>Go to the library</u>

If you live in an environment where a lot of activity goes on, then get out of that environment. Go someplace quiet where you can focus on preparing for your test.

<u>Think positive</u>

Remember when you walk into the test you have a 100 percent. It is up to you to keep it. Success is a state of mind. If you studied hard then you should feel very confident that you are going to make an A on the exam.

<u>Stay focused</u>

Stay focused and concentrate. Most tests are about one hour long. So use that one hour to completely focus on the test you are taking. Block out any thoughts that have nothing to do the with the test.

Have a plan

The most calming thing you can do for yourself is to have a plan. If you already know how you are going to approach the test, then there will be no surprises.

Have staying power

Sometimes anxiety can cause you to loose patience with what you are doing. When it comes to taking tests, you must be patient. If you do not have patience, you will just mark anything on the test whether it is right or wrong. Patience makes you sit and try to figure out the answer. Patience helps you to find the **correct answer**. Patience forces you to sit through the entire test and allows you to be one of the last people to leave. So, have patience when taking your exam.

The calming effect

Once you start the test and you take 5 minutes to write down things you might forget, you are also calming yourself down at the same time.

Anxiety

A little anxiety is good. It keeps you from feeling overconfident and decreases your chances of making unnecessary errors. Practice the above tips and you will see a considerable difference in how you feel at test time.

Conclusion

This book does not show you how to pass a test without studying. It is, instead, a book for those who do study but cannot seem to achieve the grade.

If you believe, as I do, that ***the key to success in school is knowledge of the material first, and good test-taking skills second,*** then you will definitely succeed.

You're about to get ***really, really good*** at something you thought, once upon a time, was impossible to master. You're about to ***become the straight A student*** you thought you could never be.

Thinkers

The following questions are designed to make you think.

Name four animals that start with the letter B.

1._____

2._____

3._____

4._____

Name four animals that start with the letter C.

1._____

2._____

3._____

4._____

Check answers on page 108.

Thinker

Which picture is different?

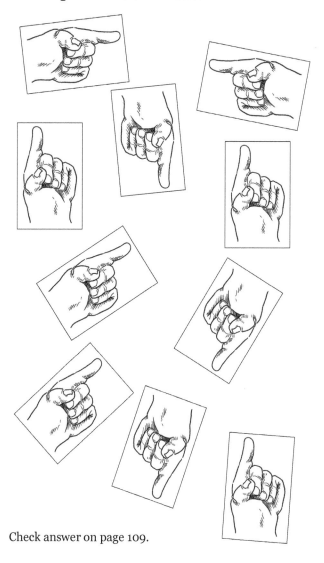

Check answer on page 109.

Thinker

Which picture is different?

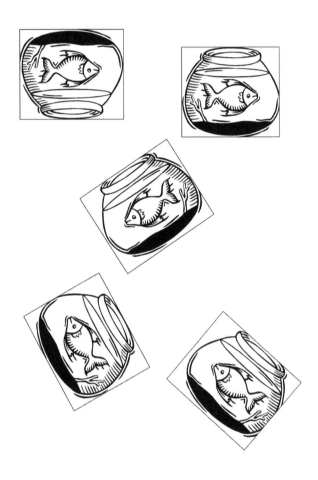

Check answer on page 109.

Thinker

1. Solve the following math problem by placing the following signs in the spaces below. There are at least two ways to solve the problem.

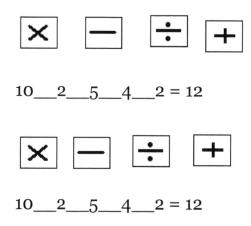

10__2__5__4__2 = 12

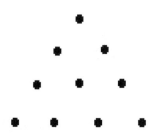

10__2__5__4__2 = 12

2. Make 9 triangles by using only 18 lines to connect the dots.

Check answers on page 110.

Answers to thinkers

From page 104.

There are many animals with names that start with the letter B or C, so here are four of them.

1. Badger

2. Bear

3. Beaver

4. Bird

Animal that names start with the letter C.

1. Camel

2. Cat

3. Cow

4. Chicken

Answers to thinkers

From page 105.

There is only one right hand, all the others are left hands.

Correct answer

From Page 106.

If you placed all of the bowls in the upright position you would see that all of the fish are facing left except for the one below. It is facing right.

Correct answer

Answers to thinkers

From Page 107.

Question 1.

$10 - 2 \times 5 \div 4 + 2 = 12$

$10 \div 2 + 5 - 4 \times 2 = 12$

Question 2.

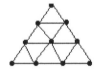

Who will benefit from this book

High School Students

College Students

Law Students

Nursing Students

Medical School Students

GED Students

Law Enforcement Students

Certified Nursing Assistants

Podiatry School Students

Optometry School Students

Graduate Students

Middle School Students

And many, many more

About the Author

Dr. D. Barnes is a graduate of the New York College of Podiatric Medicine and the University of the District of Columbia. She taught Human Anatomy and Physiology at DeKalb College's Lawrenceville campus in 1996. She was a home bound teacher for the Westchester County School System in New York for four years. She also tutored many students over the years in a vast array of subjects.

She, too, was an inferior test taker who graduated at the bottom of her high school class. She mastered the art of test taking and received the Author Webb award for academic excellence in her senior year of college and a PICA scholarship for academic excellence in her senior year of Podiatric Medical School.

She was inducted into the National Scientific Honor Society (Beta Kappa Chi) while attending the University of the District of Columbia, and the Pi Delta National Podiatric Honor society while attending the New York College of Podiatric Medicine.

CPSIA information can be obtained
at www.ICGtesting.com
Printed in the USA
LVHW050530130819
627344LV00006B/167/P